The Word WorkOut Plan

The Word WorkOut Plan

Sheldon M. Brown

Copyright © 2021 by Sheldon M. Brown.

Library of Congress Control Number:		2021921463
ISBN:	Hardcover	978-1-6641-0843-1
	Softcover	978-1-6641-0842-4
	eBook	978-1-6641-0841-7

All rights reserved. No part of this book may be reproduced or transmitted in any form or by any means, electronic or mechanical, including photocopying, recording, or by any information storage and retrieval system, without permission in writing from the copyright owner.

Scripture quotations marked KJV are from the Holy Bible, King James Version (Authorized Version). First published in 1611. Quoted from the KJV Classic Reference Bible, Copyright © 1983 by The Zondervan Corporation.

Any people depicted in stock imagery provided by Getty Images are models, and such images are being used for illustrative purposes only.
Certain stock imagery © Getty Images.

Print information available on the last page.

Rev. date: 10/18/2021

To order additional copies of this book, contact:
Xlibris
844-714-8691
www.Xlibris.com
Orders@Xlibris.com
834418

Contents

Introduction ix
Workout Gear xi
The Nutrition Plan... xv
The Workout Prayer xvii

Day 1	Faith That Moves	1
Day 2	Spiritual Warfare..	3
Day 3	I Think You Need to Cut It................................	5
Day 4	God Has the Final Say	7
Day 5	Run the Race...	9
Day 6	The Spirit of Giving	11
Day 7	It's Time to Grow Up in God.............................	13
Day 8	Just Endure	15
Day 9	Victory Belongs to Me..	17
Day 10	You've Got the Best of My Love	19
Day 11	Just Say Sorry	21
Day 12	Get Me Out of This..	23
Day 13	Living Wealthy	25
Day 14	The Power of Perseverance................................	28
Day 15	Unselfish Living..	30
Day 16	Life's Interruptions...	32
Day 17	Trying a Different Approach..............................	34
Day 18	Move Your Feet, Not Just Your Mouth...................	36
Day 19	The Process of the Prophecy	38
Day 20	A Messed Up Mindset	40

Day 21	As for Me and My House	42
Day 22	The Ultimate Sacrifice	44
Day 23	I Was Created to Worship	46
Day 24	Spoiled by My Daddy	48
Day 25	A Servant's Heart	50
Day 26	Holiness Is Still Right	52
Day 27	Thank God for My Angels	54
Day 28	My Hiding Place	56
Day 29	The Apple of My Eye	58
Day 30	I Smile	60
Day 31	Happiness versus Joy	62
Day 32	Open Your Mouth	64
Day 33	Watch Your Tongue	66
Day 34	Am I Still Your Number 1?	68
Day 35	A Mind Takeover	70
Day 36	A Savior Who Satisfies	72
Day 37	The Power of Consistency	74
Day 38	Shine a Light on 'Em	76
Day 39	Can't Touch This	78
Day 40	Can You Handle the Truth?	80

The Salvation Plan	83
I Am a King!	85
Acknowledgments	87
For Booking	89

This book is dedicated to my beautiful black queen, Michelle Brown, and my three handsome young black kings—Zion Brown (eleven), Zaire Brown (nine), Zuriel Brown (six)—and the young prince, Zayden Brown. They have given me the push and the drive to birth out this great accomplishment.

I also dedicate this book to all five of my deceased grandparents—the late William and Sandora Bouyer, the late Harry and Elise Brown (a.k.a. the Brown Singers), and Mother Annie Allen, for her spiritual wisdom and guidance.

Introduction

This book was written to encourage the believer and nonbeliever and to give motivational words of the day that will uplift, motivate, and captivate those who want to work out their soul's salvation and grow daily with God. *The Word Workout Plan* was inspired by years of daily Facebook Word of the Days, the Prayer Room Ministry, and years of Friday- and Saturday-night live prayer and was governed by the Holy Spirit.

I pray that after you have read this book that your spiritual muscles will have grown and matured in God. Working out is a consistent process, and when it's done daily, it produces much growth and much success. When you work out your natural muscles, there is a process. There is truth, there is pain, there is progression, and there is pleasure. Each one of these plays a very important role in the Word workout plan. As you journey through the Word workout plan, note that if you want to build spiritual muscles, if you want to lose negative energy and spiritual weight, you have to allow God to open your heart and your spirit to receive what the Holy Spirit is teaching you through it.

The scripture says that Jesus went into the wilderness for forty days, fasted, and was hungry, and the devil tempted him (Luke 4:1–13). You are led to do your forty-day workout plan that's between you and God. However, just know that the devil is going to tempt you and try to get you offtrack, but I challenge you to keep working out, no matter how bad it hurts or no matter what you have to endure. God is the author and finisher of the Word workout plan. I just wrote the book.

It's a good day for a workout!

Workout Gear

Workout clothing is designed for a specific purpose: protection from the environment. If it gets too hot, shorts should be worn, and if it gets too cold, long pants and thick layers of clothing should be applied. Workout gear can provide comfort and can improve your range of motion. Your clothing plays a pretty big part of your workout performance. Before you start your forty-day workout plan, make sure you have on the right clothes.

> Put on the whole armour of God, that you may be able to stand the wiles of the devil. For we wrestle not against flesh and blood but fight against principalities, against powers, against rulers of the darkness of this world and against spiritual wickedness in high places. (Ephesians 6:11–12)

The helmet of salvation is worn to guard your mind.

- As you work out, focus and don't get distracted or sidetracked. You have a goal in mind.

The breastplate of righteousness is worn to guard your heart and to cover it with the will to do right.

- As you are working out, you will encounter challenges that will try to change your heart. Allow God to fix your heart and cover it with righteousness.

The belt of truth is worn to hold you up with the truth even when you feel defeated.

- When you are working out, there are some things that are going to be hard to accept about yourself, but let the truth wrap itself around you and embrace it.

The shield of faith is used for your protection against the devil and your haters who want to see you fail.

- I told you before that just as Jesus was tempted, you will be also, but you have to apply your faith and trust that no weapon formed against you will prosper (Isaiah 54:17). Let God deal with it!

The sword of the Spirit is the Word of God, and when it is applied to your daily life, it will cut and kill out everything that is not of God.

- I think that one is pretty simple. You have to let the Word do what it was sent out in your life to do. Read the Word and apply it, because when you are hearers only and not doers, you lie to yourself (James 1:22–25).

Lastly, get yourself some fresh Jordans or Nikes and call them your shoes of peace.

- As you work out, there are some surfaces that are going to be smooth and some that may be a little rough, but keep your steps ordered with the peace of God, knowing that all things are working for God (Romans 8:28).

Put your clothes on!

The Nutrition Plan

O taste and see that the Lord is good.
—Psalm 34:8

During this workout plan, you must make sure that you are well nourished. You have to feed your spirit every scripture and prayer that is presented in the workout plan. *You must eat him to become him.* The Word is your daily supplement, the Word is your source of nutrition, and the Word is even your daily bread. Your spirit has to experience the goodness of God.

The Workout Prayer

God, today I pray for strength. It's been a long time since I have worked out with your Word. I pray that I lose every weight and sin that keeps me bound. I pray that you will give me an unquenchable appetite for you and your Word like never before. When I run, please, Lord, don't let me get tired, out of breath, and want to give up. Give me your Holy Spirit to keep my body energized and my thirst quenched one day at a time. In Jesus's mighty name, amen.

I'm all ready for a good workout!

Day 1

Word of the Day

FAITH THAT MOVES

God has given every one of us a destiny, a vision, and a divine assignment. In order to fulfill that assignment, we must have faith that moves. We cannot just talk about what we want for our lives, but we must move our faith. We have to *put some feet on our faith* and trust God and go get what God has for us. Don't just move your lips but move your mind. Move your goals and move your faith. Faith without movement is no good. So today I challenge you to get up and move. Write your book. Go back to school. Get your GED. Start your business. Whatever you do, you gotta get up and move and do it now. The world is waiting on the next best thing, and that next thing is you.

Prayer

Dear God, help me to move my faith. I understand that faith without works is dead (James 2:14–26). I want to live out the calling in my life. God, please be my guide and help me put my faith into action. Help me to move my faith and not just my mouth. Amen.

#NowFaith

#FaithThatMoves

#MoveMeGod

Word Workout Plan

Hebrews 11:1–6 KJV

1 Thessalonians 2:13 KJV

John 20:27 KJV

James 2:14–26 KJV

Day 2

Word of the Day

SPIRITUAL WARFARE

Spiritual warfare is the Christian concept of fighting against the work of preternatural (beyond what is natural) evil forces. It is out of the ordinary, rare, unusual, and uncommon. *We cannot sleepwalk. We must be well aware of the things that we cannot see.* This thing goes far beyond your local church, far beyond a church anniversary, and well past a Wednesday-night Bible study.

Today we must understand that some of the things we fight against are not always natural but some things are spiritual. We fight in our minds, we fight in our hearts, we fight in our flesh, and we also fight in our everyday walk with God. Spiritual warfare is understanding that some things we go through in life are caused by evil forces that have been assigned to try and destroy our lives, wreak havoc, and cause us to miss every blessing that God has for us. God has already given us the victory. So today, walk in that victory and let God fight your battles.

#FightFightFight

#KeepFighting

Prayer

God, help me to fight the daily thoughts that pass through my mind. Give me the strength to overcome those battles and the struggles that I fight every day. Amen.

Word Workout Plan

Ephesians 6:10–12 KJV

James 4:7 KJV

2 Corinthians 10:4–6

Day 3

Word of the Day

I THINK YOU NEED TO CUT IT

We all have something that we give our attention to more than the things that should have our main focus—a friend, a job, or maybe an abusive relationship. Someone may be addicted to drugs or alcohol or experiencing a sexual addiction.

Something or someone is taking our full attention off God and all the blessings that he wants to give. Today it's time to cut it. *It's taking too much of your time and energy*, and you need to get your focus back. God has so many blessings he wants to give you, but first, I think you need to cut it!

\#SoCalledFriends

\#GetYourFocusBack

\#GodHasMoreForYou

\#ItIsTimeToCutIt

Prayer

Today, for everything in my life that is causing me disconnection from God and all his blessings, I pray that God would give me the strength to delete and remove them out of my life for good. Amen.

Word Workout Plan

Psalm 34:17

James 5:16

Galatians 5:1

John 8:32

Romans 6:14–19

Day 4

Word of the Day

GOD HAS THE FINAL SAY

Be careful who you let speak into your life. Be careful who you even let pray over you. We possess the power to pronounce blessings or curses over somebody's life.

Make a choice to speak blessings and not curses. Regardless of what people try to say about you or do to you, God has the final say over your life. Ask Job. He will tell you that his wife wanted him to curse God and die because of all that he was going through, but at the end of the day, God still had the final say. Job trusted God. Job did not give into what people said about him or thought of him. He lost a whole lot but gained more favor with God, and God gave him double for all his trouble. God knew that he would never turn his back on Job, but Satan had to try to tempt him, and he lost. *God's yes is always bigger than the devil's no.* As long as God has the final say, you are in good hands.

#WatchYourMouth

#TrustGod

#GodGotIt

Prayer

God, order my steps so that the devil gets no say over my life. In Jesus's name, amen.

Word Workout Plan

Proverbs 18:21 KJV

Luke 6:45 KJV

Proverbs 13:3

Day 5

Word of the Day

RUN THE RACE

Imagine that you are in a race, and as you are running, there are so many obstacles and many hurdles that try to hinder you from finishing or getting to your goal. That's how life is. In life, you are going to have many trials and many obstacles, but you gotta keep running. Don't stop! Keep your mind centered on God, and he will give you the strength to jump every hurdle, to climb every mountain, and to overcome every obstacle in your life. When you get tired and feel like you can't go on anymore, pass the baton to Jesus, lay it on the altar, and let him work it out. This race is different because we already have the victory! What a feeling it is when you are running a race and you cross that finish line. What an even greater joy it is when you cross that line in first place. *Run your race with the first place in your view.*

#KeepRunning

#YouGotThis

#PassTheBatonToJesus

Prayer

Lord, help me every day to run a race that is pleasing to you and, when I get tired, to lay it all at your feet. In Jesus's name, amen.

Word Workout Plan

Hebrews 12:1–2 KJV

Philippians 3:14 KJV

1 Corinthians 9:24–27 KJV

Philippians 2:16

Day 6

Word of the Day

THE SPIRIT OF GIVING

Having a spirit of giving causes God's hand to move on your behalf. *The more you give, the more God graciously gives to you.* You cannot only give to God and the ministry but you can also give to the unhoused, the less fortunate, and those who are in need. Having a spirit of giving can also prompt you to even pay for someone's gas or pay for someone's meal in the drive-through line at McDonald's. Give of your time, your treasures, and your talents and watch God's blessing overtake you. Give! Give of your time, give of your talents, and give of your finances and watch the windows of heaven fly open for you. Get your buckets ready because God is going to pour out rivers of blessings on you. You can't beat God's giving no matter how hard you try.

#GiveAndItWillComeBackToYou

Prayer

God, today I pray that you would help me to be selfless and not selfish. Help me to be a giver so that I can receive numerous blessings from you. I was called to be a giver. In Jesus's name, amen.

Word Workout Plan

Luke 6:38 KJV

Proverbs 18:16 NIV

Proverbs 11:25 NIV

Proverbs 3:9 NIV

Malachi 3:6–12 KJV

Day 7

Word of the Day

IT'S TIME TO GROW UP IN GOD

When we are babies in Christ, everything that we do stems from the mentality of an infinite—how we pray, how we praise, how we worship, and how we have such a carnal way of thinking. We are lovers of immature activities and pleasures more than lovers of God and the things of God. *There comes a time when we must put away our childish mentality* and grow up and start maturing in life as well as our praise and worship. Go the extra mile and let God take full control over you. Start going deeper in God's Word. Ask God for deeper revelation. Pray more, praise more, and worship God more than you ever have. It's time to grow up in God.

Prayer

God, help me to grow up spiritually and mature in my walk with you. Amen.

#GrowUp

#INeedMore

#TheTimeIsNow

#MaturityLooksGoodOnMe!

Word Workout Plan

1 Corinthians 14:20 KJV

1 Corinthians 3:1–3 KJV

Galatians 5:22–23

2 Thessalonians 1:3

Day 8

Word of the Day

JUST ENDURE

So many times in life, we get weighed down by the things of this life. Things get hard. Money gets funny, and sometimes your change gets a little strange. Bills start piling up. The cares of life will have you wondering where God is in all this. Have you ever felt like giving up because of situations around you? So many deaths and sickness and so much going on. COVID-19 has left us with so many scares that only God can heal. Well, today I challenge you to just endure. *Enduring* is a verb that means "to remain in existence no matter what." A *verb* is an action word. *When you endure, you put faith in action.* Don't give up. Don't give in. Just endure. You got this.

Prayer

Lord, help me even when I want to give up and throw in the towel. Help me to endure whatever comes my way and help me to learn from every stumbling block that life brings. In Jesus's name, amen.

#HelpMeJesus

#INeedYouNow

#JustEndure

Word Workout Plan

2 Chronicles 15:7 KJV

Isaiah 41:10

Hebrews 12:1–3

Philippians 3:7–14

Day 9

Word of the Day

VICTORY BELONGS TO ME

Today, activate your faith. Start speaking of victory. Speak of your healing and speak of setting yourself free. Your words have power. Christ died so that we could have access to everything in heaven and on earth. Call forth what you want to see happen in your life and watch the manifestation of it come to pass. Use your faith and let God do the rest. You were created to walk in victory. Victory belongs to you.

#VictoryIsMine

Prayer

God, help me change my language. Help me to start claiming and speaking of what's rightfully mine. Amen.

Word Workout Plan

Proverbs 18:21 KJV

Matthew 21:22 KJV

Isaiah 55:11 KJV

Mark 4:4 KJV

Romans 4:17 KJV

Day 10

Word of the Day

YOU'VE GOT THE BEST OF MY LOVE

God gave us his best when he gave us Jesus Christ. God allowed him to take on the worst death so that we may live our best life. His life is the greatest demonstration of love—that a man would lay down his life for his friend. *God gave us a gift that money can't buy.* Love was hung on a tree. Love was nailed to a cross. Love died and rose. And love is coming back again for those who love him. Jesus is love, and he demonstrates his love to us every day. His love gives us a new mercy. His love graces us to get up each and every day. His love forgives even when we are wrong, and his love is enough to hurt us with the truth just to heal us from ourselves.

Prayer

God, thank you for your love that you give to me each and every day. I thank you for your great demonstration of love at the Calvary when you sent your only Son to die so that I may live.

#LoveLiveLearn

Word Workout Plan

John 3:16 KJV

1 Corinthians 13 KJV

John 13:34–35 KJV

Day 11

Word of the Day

JUST SAY SORRY

In life, we sometimes never want to admit when we are wrong. We tend to suppress the truth rather than just own up to our mistakes and just say sorry. *Sometimes we have to become low so that we can fly high.* Sometimes we just have to humble ourselves, not only in God but also in life. Life sometimes requires us to take the back seat and eat humble pie all for the greater good. Most of the time, you can avoid major confrontation just by confessing that you were wrong and that you're sorry.

This subject I know oh so well being a happily married man. I have avoided nights being mad at each other, not speaking for days, or even looking at each other sideways at public events just by saying, "Babe, I'm sorry." Call it what you want, but sorry goes a long way. Even God himself says that if you just confess your sins, he is faithful to forgive you of your sins and to cleanse you from all your unrighteousness (1 John 1:9). God said that!

The bottom line is to just say sorry.

#IAmSorry

#ForgiveMe

#Higher

#BabeIAmSorry

#MarriedLife

Prayer

God, help me to accept my faults and my wrongs and keep me humble.

Word Workout Plan

Matthew 5:23–24

James 5:16

Proverbs 10:12

Luke 17:3–4

Day 12

Word of the Day

GET ME OUT OF THIS

Have you ever gotten yourself into something that had you so far gone that you even compromised who you were and all that you stood for? I have! We all have prayed this prayer, "God, if you just get me out of this, I promise to never do it again." *Life can present so many bad opportunities that if you let it, it can leave you blind* to the things of God, blind to what's good for your well-being, blind to what's good for your family, blind to what people are going to say, blind to all you have worked for and become. Yes, even blind to having a good name for yourself. Shoot! I found myself in every one of these areas, but that will be in my next book. (Stay tuned.) Shoot! I really needed God to be an eye doctor because I just could not see clearly. Well, today, my brothers and my sisters, God has given you another opportunity to come out of what you are in and give your entire life back to him.

Get right or get left. I was blind, but now I see.

#GetMeOutJesus

#GetRightOrGetLeft

#GiveItUp

#JesusBeAnEyeDoctorLOL

Prayer

Lord, please help me to be free from the things that have me bound.

Word Workout Plan

Galatians 5:1

Isaiah 43:18–19

Romans 6:14–19

2 Corinthians 6:17

Day 13

Word of the Day

LIVING WEALTHY

Living wealthy can be a great blessing or can become your biggest nightmare. How? Well, I'm glad you asked. It's so nice to have big houses and drive fancy cars. It's nice to be chauffeured and not have to worry about driving to major events. It's even a blessing when you can shop till you drop and buy the latest fashion. But what would happen to you if one day all that was gone? Would you still have your integrity? Would you still have faith and trust in God? Being wealthy is not just having money alone. *You can have all the money in the world and still be poor* spiritually, mentally, physically, or emotionally. Being wealthy is thanking God every day that your family is taken care of. Being wealthy is thanking God that you are in good health because somebody somewhere can hardly get out of bed. Being wealthy is being in your right mind, being able to make your own decisions and not being brain-dead or unconscious, having the activity of your limbs, and being able to move on your own. You might be using a cane, but you're walking. Being wealthy is having family and friends who love and support and care about your well-being.

Today, thank God for your wealth and the things in life that we take for granted every day. It's hard for a rich man to inherit the kingdom of God because sometimes we think, *Why do I need God if I have everything already?* But I say if I lost everything and still have Jesus, it would be enough to start all over again.

#NotAlwaysInMoney

#SafeInHisArms

#WealthBelongsToMe

Prayer

God, help me to thank you for the wealth you have already given me and prepare me to receive the wealth that's about to come into my life. Amen.

Word Workout Plan

Mark 10:25

Hebrews 13:5

Proverbs 10:4

Matthew 19:24

James 5:1–6

Matthew 6:21

Revelations

Luke 16:19–21

Day 14

Word of the Day

THE POWER OF PERSEVERANCE

This is not the time to give up! This is not the time to tuck tail and run! This is not the time to give in to temptation. We are too close to the coming of Jesus. We are too close to the rapture. What sense does it make to throw in the towel now after you have fasted? After you have prayed? After you have cried? After you have shouted like a fool for Jesus? Some of us had to give up some friends. Some of us had to change some phone numbers. Some of us had to be lied to. Some of us had to be talked about. Yes, even stabbed in our backs. But today I push you to persevere! You have an inherited power from Jesus himself, and I don't care what is going on in your life. Keep going, don't give up, and don't give in. You were anointed to finish, so *finish with faith and finish strong.*

\#IAmGoingAllTheWay

\#NotTheTimeToGiveUp

\#IJustCan'tFinishNow

Prayer

God, whatever it may be, give me the strength to stick to it and persevere. Amen.

Word Workout Plan

Ecclesiastes 9:11

Galatians 6:9

Revelations 2:10

James 1:12

Day 15

Word of the Day

UNSELFISH LIVING

Learn how to give of yourself unselfishly, not always for your own personal gain but to benefit the needs of others. Let's make every day a day of unselfish living—pay for someone's meal in the drive-through line, be a blessing to someone with a cash app, pick up the phone and encourage somebody other than yourself. Yes, even give to that homeless person on the street whom you feel is faking, and you even see his fresh Jordans on his feet. I have learned in life that regardless of whatever I'm striving to get my crown of life, I'm storing up treasures in heaven when I am not on earth. God never said to give to those whom you don't think are faking; God just said to give. You never know, in your giving, you might be able to say a short prayer and save their soul or make them come off the counter. We all are important to the body of Christ.

Today, *let's put down ourselves and pick up salvation* because Jesus gave his all for everybody—the sinner, the drug addict, the prostitute, the alcoholic, the stripper, the homosexual, the lesbian, and yes, even you, my friend.

#IGiveMyselfAway

#ForYourGlory

#NotMyWillButYours

Prayer

Lord, help me to give myself away so that you can use me for your glory. Amen.

Word Workout Plan

Galatians 3:34

2 Corinthians 8:9

Isaiah 53:3–12

Luke 6:38

Day 16

Word of the Day

LIFE'S INTERRUPTIONS

Don't let life's interruptions interrupt the plans and the assignments that God has for your life. The devil will try his best to bring many interferences and disturbances to steer you off your course. He wants your dream and goals to come to a halt. He wants you to cease from excelling in life. Don't let life get the best out of you; you get the best out of the life God has given you. Interrupt the devil's plans by giving God the praise and interrupt the devil's goal to get you to worry with worship. Sometimes you have to shout through it. Praise your way through.

There have been many times in my life where I had major life interruptions that were beyond my control. I just have to give it to God and let him work it out literally. In the meantime, I never, *never ever* lost my praise. Praise had gotten me through the hardest times in my life. Just trust and believe in God for a turnaround. You might say, "Well, it does not take all that." But as the songwriter wrote, "You don't know my story and all the things that I've been through. You can't feel my pain and what I had to go through to get here." You'll never understand my praise, so don't try to figure it out. All you need to know is that my worship and my praise are for real. *Nope! Not today, devil.* We interrupt this regularly scheduled program with praise!

#PutAPraiseOnIt

#IStillHaveJoy

#KeepItMoving

#NotTodayDevil!

Prayer

God, today I say goodbye to looking at life's interruptions as setbacks and using them as excuses. Today I embrace my new mindset and my new way of approaching life. Amen.

Word Workout Plan

1 Corinthians 9:21

James 1:12

Philippians 4:13

Colossians 3:23–24

Day 17

Word of the Day

TRYING A DIFFERENT APPROACH

So today I watched the classic movie *Sister Act*. In the movie, we find ourselves in a traditional Roman Catholic Church, but the church is not growing and not prospering. The nuns where unexpectedly blessed with a new nun, and she began to try a different approach. When she steps out on faith, the church begins to thrive, the attendance skyrockets, and the people in the community and the local church get more involved. Don't miss your blessing because you're in your own way. God wants to do a new thing in you and for you, but *sometimes you gotta get out of your own way*. Step back and let God do it his way. We even think God needs our assistance or our way is better than God's way. Sometimes we even think God has lost his everlasting mind, but he hasn't. The bottom line is, sometimes you gotta *try a different approach.*

#GodIsDoingANewThing

#ADifferentApproach

#UseMeLord

Prayer

God, today help me not to get so stuck on the traditions and my everyday things that I miss out on a new move of God. Lord, do a new thing in me. Amen.

Word Workout Plan

Ezekiel 11:19

Isaiah 42:10

Jeremiah 31:22

Isaiah 55:8–9

Revelations 21:5

Day 18

Word of the Day

MOVE YOUR FEET, NOT JUST YOUR MOUTH

In the world we live in today, we have a lot of people talking about their hopes, dreams, goals, and everything that they want to do in their lifetime. They are always blabbing about the many opportunities that they want to do, the many places they want to visit, the big houses they want to live in, and yes, even the car that they want to drive. One of the richest places is the grave. Graves are filled with people who died with million-dollar ideas and inventions and books and novels that could have changed the entire world. I challenge you to *put some feet on your faith* and go get what God has for you. Don't just talk about the book you want to write. Write it! Don't just talk about going back to school. Apply for classes and go get your degree. It is your time and your turn. Go get it!

#GoGetIt

#StopAllThatTalkingAndStartWalking

#LetYourFeetDoTheTalkingThisTime

Prayer

God, help me to get my feet motivated and not just my mouth. I want to do your will and accomplish what you have for me, so, Lord, help me to bind up the spirit of procrastination. Amen.

Word Workout Plan

Ecclesiastes 9:10

Ecclesiastes 11:4

Galatians 6:9

Hebrews 12:1

Day 19

Word of the Day

THE PROCESS OF THE PROPHECY

When God gives us a word or when God speaks to us through someone, we jump, we shout, and we praise God. But what we sometimes forget is that there is a process for your prophecy. God might give us a word, and it does not come to pass until years later. There is a process that everyone must go through before the Word of the Lord becomes manifested in your life. *The prophecy might not find you until you are at your lowest point in your life.* It could even very well find you when you think that you have arrived and are doing well. The process may not be pleasant or grand, but just know that it's going to work out for your good.

\#ThereIsAProcess

\#ItsWorkingForYourGood

\#GoThroughWithGrace

Prayer

God, prepare me for my process. Give me the strength to endure hardship as a good soldier as I wait for your blessings to manifest in my life. Amen.

Word Workout Plan

Romans 8:28

Hebrews 4:12

1 Thessalonians 2:13

Isaiah 55:11

2 Timothy 2:3–5

Matthew 4:4

Day 20

Word of the Day

A MESSED UP MINDSET

As believers, we must allow God to take full control over our minds. We must not give our thoughts over to negativity, fear, depression, or suicidal thoughts. If we do, we have allowed our minds to be contaminated and messed up not only by the enemy but also by people and their opinions and perceptions about us. Just think. What if you lived your life based on what people thought about you? Yep, I did that too! Guilty. I always used to think what people would say or think if I did that. *I lived my life for people until I realized that's not living at all.* I want to remind you today that God is fully capable of turning our mess into a miracle. Change the way you think and start speaking positivity into and over your life. Speak of blessings.

#ThinkPositive

#BlessingOnBlessing

#HeCanAndHeWill

Prayer

Lord, today I am asking you to help me change my messed-up mindset. I want to think and live more in the blessings of life versus life's difficulties. Amen.

Word Workout Plan

Isaiah 26:3

Colossians 3:2

Matthew 22:37

Proverbs 27:17

Day 21

Word of the Day

AS FOR ME AND MY HOUSE

So many people are born into or choose to serve the god of their choice. There are so many religions, so many higher powers, so many man upstairs. But as for me and my house, we will serve the Lord Jesus Christ. There is only one god who sent his Son to die for the sins of the entire world. Jesus is the only god who is 100 percent god and 100 percent man. Jesus is the only god who can deliver our souls from eternal damnation. I'll take Jesus over every other god there is. Jesus saves, Jesus heals, and Jesus sets free. *My entire house and I will serve the Lord Jesus Christ.*

#IWillServeTheLord

#Joshua24:15

\#JesusSaves

\#IAmSaveda

Prayer

God, today I surrender my life to you. I give you my mind, body, soul, and heart. I vow to live a life that pleases you. I believe that you sent your Son to die for my sins and rose from the grave. In Jesus's name, amen.

Word Workout Plan

Joshua 24:15

Romans 10:9

Romans 12:11

Colossians 3:23–24

Day 22

Word of the Day

THE ULTIMATE SACRIFICE

At his age of thirty-three, Jesus Christ made the ultimate sacrifice. The price was paid, and our sins were atoned. The sacrificial lamb had made intercessions for the sins of the whole world through his own blood. What sacrifice have you made for God today? What have you given up or taken on to please God? What can you offer to God today? What about spending more time with him? What about giving your talents or maybe more of your treasures? *Really, God just wants your heart, and everything else will follow.* Love him with your whole heart.

Prayer

God, help me to give more of me to you. Help my love for you to reflect my life of sacrifice. Amen.

Word Workout Plan

Psalm 51:17

Romans 12:1

John 3:16–18

Hebrew 13:16

Romans 3:35

1 Samuel 15:22

Day 23

Word of the Day

I WAS CREATED TO WORSHIP

In life, we try to find our goals, our destiny, and our purpose for existing. We search for our dreams to become reality and expect them to lead us to great success, and we believe that's what we were born to do. Well, today I challenge you to rethink your reason for being created. We were created to love God first and worship and serve him only, and everything else will fall right into place. *I was created to be a worshipper.*

#IAmAWorshipper

#Worship1st

#God1st

Prayer

God, help me to reposition my life and put you back first as lord over my life. Amen.

Word Workout Plan

Revelations 4:9–11

Isaiah 43:7

Genesis 2:4–17

Isaiah 25:1

Day 24

Word of the Day

SPOILED BY MY DADDY

What shall we say then? If our daddy is for us, it's more than the whole world against us. Some of us deal with the reality of our nature fathers not being present in our lives or may not feel accepted by our nature father. Maybe you try and try to live up to your nature father's standards and fall every time. Today I want to introduce you to my daddy. He is the Father of fathers. His love for me is out of this world, and he spoils the heck out of his children who love him and trust him. *He can be whatever you need him to be*—a mother, a brother, a sister, or a friend. But to me, he is my daddy.

#Daddy

#Father

#Spoiled

#WellTakenCareOf

#Daddy'sBoy

#Daddy'sGirl

Prayer

Daddy, thank you for filling the void in my life that was left because of the absence of my nature father. You're a good, good Father. Amen.

Word Workout Plan

1 John 3:1

Proverbs 3:11–12

Matthew 6:6, 26

John 10:28–30

Proverbs 15:15

John 14:23

Day 25

Word of the Day

A SERVANT'S HEART

Having a servant's heart requires humility, taking the back seat sometimes, not always wanting to be seen. *A servant's heart is filled with compassion and love.* The heart is the rhythm and the beat of the body, not just for the physical body but also the spiritual body. God is looking for someone who has a heart after him. As believers, we must have a heart to serve the Lord and not be ashamed.

#AServant'sHeart

#Compassion

#AHeartLikeGod

#Humble

Prayer

God, create in me a heart that longs for you.

Word Workout Plan

Hebrews 6:10

John 12:26

1 Corinthians 28:9

Matthew 23:11

Mark 10:45

Day 26

Word of the Day

HOLINESS IS STILL RIGHT

Living a holy life nowadays seems so irrelevant. People just seem to think living and doing whatever they want is okay. They pray and ask God to give them grace, mercy, and forgiveness and then go right back and do the same thing over and over again. Living holy may not seem fun, may seem unnecessary, or may seem like there is no point, but at the end of the day, there is a way that may seem right yet will lead to destruction. You can be saved and sexy and not have to come out of character. You can be hopeful and holy and not have to live the life of a harlot. You can be a caring Christian and not seem like a punk. Christianity is about being like Christ. Christ lived a holy life. The world gravitated to him by the millions, and the world is still gravitating to him today. *Get right or get left!*

#HolyLiving

#SaveAndSanctified

#ChristLike

#BeHoly4IAmHoly

Prayer

God, help me to walk out this Christian journey and to live a life that pleases you. Amen.

Word Workout Plan

Deuteronomy 7:6

Deuteronomy 26:18–19

Leviticus 20:26

1 Peter 1:15–16

Day 27

Word of the Day

THANK GOD FOR MY ANGELS

What are angels? An *angel* is a supernatural being used in various religions. Angels are used as God's helpers on earth. Angels watch over us when we are asleep. Angels ward off spiritual beings that try to do us harm, and angels even show up and bring us news of what's to come. *Thank God for my angels of protection who shield and protect me from the evil in this world.* Thank God for the angels in my life who show up and send blessings unexpectedly. Thank God for my angels.

#AngelsAreReal

#ThankGod

#TheyAreWatchingOverMe

Prayer

Father, I thank you for my angels who you send to watch over me every day. Amen.

Word Workout Plan

Psalm 91:11

Revelations 4:8, 14:6

1 Peter 1:2

Isaiah 14:12–19

Day 28

Word of the Day

MY HIDING PLACE

When life comes at me hard, when I am frustrated, when I am stressed, when I am uneasy about the things that I am doing, when finances are an issue, when church folk get on my nerves, when my spouse is acting up, and when the world is going crazy, there is a hiding place that I can go to. There is peace. There is joy. There is love. There is everything that I need in my hiding place. When the storms of life hit me hard, I can hide and rest in him. *The Word of God is my hiding place, and I can take refuge in his Word.*

#HideMeInYourWord

#RestInGod

#IFindPeaceInHim

Prayer

Lord, help me to take refuge in your Word, and when the struggle becomes real, I can rest in you because you're a real god.

Word Workout Plan

Psalm 91

Psalm 32:7

Psalm 119:114

Psalm 61:3

Psalm 31:20

Day 29

Word of the Day

THE APPLE OF MY EYE

The phrase "apple of my eye" refers to someone or something you love and cherish above all else. Sometimes we say that our spouses or boyfriend or girlfriend are the apple of our eyes, but have you ever considered Jesus being the apple of your eye? Loving him, cherishing him, adoring him above all else? Spending time with him more than Facebook, more than TikTok, more than Twitter? They say an apple a day keeps the doctor away. Well, today I'm changing it. Jesus is the apple, and today, take a bite of him because an apple a day keeps Satan away.

O taste and see that the Lord is good. (Psalm 34:8)

#TheAppleOfTheEye

#ILoveHim

#Jesus

#IPutYouFirst

Prayer

God, allow me to move everything out of the way and put you first.

Word Workout Plan

Matthew 22:37

Proverbs 3:6

Matthew 6:33

Matthew 6:19–21

Day 30

Word of the Day

I SMILE

So many times in life, we parade around and act like everything is all right. We act like we got it all together. We sometimes smile just to cover up the pain that we are really feeling inside. Somebody might be smiling at work and not know where their next meal is coming from. Somebody might be smiling at church and really not have a place to lay their head. Somebody might even be smiling at home and be suffering from depression, insecurity, or anxiety. Don't let a smile fool you. God looks beyond your smile and sees your heart. Today I made an exchange. Exchange pain for praise. Exchange your phoniness for realness and authenticity. I am who God says I am for real. *Start smiling for real*. I smile for real.

\#Smile

\#YouLookBetterWhenYouSmile4Real

\#HappyInJesus

Prayer

God, help me to find the good out of everything that I go through in life. Amen.

Word Workout Plan

Romans 8:28

Romans 15:3

James 1:2–3

1 Peter 1:8–9

Day 31

Word of the Day

HAPPINESS VERSUS JOY

There is a difference between being happy and having joy. Happiness can change depending on how we feel in the moment, but joy is everlasting no matter how we are feeling. *Happiness says, "I'm happy with my job." But joy says, "Even if I lost my job, I will still serve the Lord and have joy."* Happiness can change based on our current situations, but joy goes far beyond what the naturel eye can see. Joy goes beyond what the mind can even comprehend and far beyond what this world can even imagine. Don't let your emotions govern your spirit, but let your spirit govern your emotions. I got the joy of the Lord living inside of me.

\#IStillHaveJoy

\#HeGaveMeJoy

\#YesIGotJoy

Prayer

God, today I pray that you would give me the joy of the Lord way down deep in my soul. Amen.

Word Workout Plan

Nehemiah 8:10

1 Thessalonians 5:16–18

Philippians 4:4–11

Psalm 126:2–3

Romans 15:13

Day 32

Word of the Day

OPEN YOUR MOUTH

In the Bible, there is a story about a man named Joshua and how he won the battle at Jericho. The walls of Jericho came crashing down after Joshua's Israelite army marched around the city, blowing trumpets and using their mouths to make loud sounds as instructed by God. In life, there are some battles that cannot be won until you open your mouth and give God the praises that is due unto him. *Let praises ring from your mouth.* Let worship flow from your belly. We have been too quiet for a long time. It's time to open our big mouths and give our big God a big praise. Make a joyful noise to God and watch those walls in your life come crashing down.

\#NoWalls

\#PraiseIsWhatWeDo

\#ShoutItDown

\#FollowTheLeader

Prayer

God, today I ask that you would open my ears to hear your instructions and to allow my mouth to flow with praise so that I can be free from the things that try to block me from all my blessings. Amen.

Word Workout Plan

Joshua 6:1–27

Psalm 100

1 Peter 4:11

Deuteronomy 10:21

Day 33

Word of the Day

WATCH YOUR TONGUE

We have the power to speak change, positivity, health, and wealth into our very own atmosphere. *We can speak the change we want to see.* That little instrument called a tongue is a powerful weapon that can make your life better or bitter. We can use our tongue to speak good or evil into our lives as well as the lives of others. Watch how you use your instrument. Watch your tongue.

#WatchYourMouth

#WatchYourTongue

#SpeakIt

#IGotThePower

#GovernYourGumsLOL

Prayer

God, today I pray that you will give me the strength to watch my mouth and to only speak positivity into my life. Amen.

Word Workout Plan

1 Peter 3:10

Colossians 4:6

Psalm 141:3

Psalm 34:13

Day 34

Word of the Day

AM I STILL YOUR NUMBER 1?

In the life of being married, we sometimes get so busy with taking care of the kids, working, going to school, or maybe just our everyday living that we sometimes have to stop what we are doing and ask our spouse if I we still their number 1. Sometimes we even put social media or our phones, even our careers, in front of the person whom we said "I do" to. It often makes that person question our loyalty. It's the same way with God. *Is he still number 1 in your life, or do we put everything in front of him?* Put God first and watch what he does in your life.

#Number1

#MyFirstLove

#HeIsOnTop

Prayer

God, help me to put you first before everything I do in my life. Amen.

Word Workout Plan

Matthew 10:38–39

Matthew 22:37–40

Ephesians 20:3

Exodus 20:3

Proverbs 3:9–10

Day 35

Word of the Day

A MIND TAKEOVER

There are some people who love being in control. They love to control how their day will go. They love to be in control of their jobs. Even in marriage, they love having the upper hand and being in control. Yes, even in the church, people have a need to be in control. *It becomes a problem when we won't submit to the authority of Christ in our lives.* When we allow God to take over our minds and have full control, we surrender our will for his, our thoughts for his thoughts, our agendas for his, even our ways for his. We die to ourselves to have a new life in him. Let God take over your mind, and you will find that it is much easier doing it in God's way.

#DyingToLive

#Submit

#Surrender

#StepAside

Prayer

God, today I ask that you help me not to be in control of everything in my life. I ask that you take full control and help me to submit to your will and purpose for my life. Amen.

Word Workout Plan

Romans 12:2

Ephesians 4:22–32

Philippians 4:8

Romans 7:25–26

Isaiah 55:8–13

Day 36

Word of the Day

A SAVIOR WHO SATISFIES

As people, we often look for things, great achievements, men, women, cars, houses, and yes, even sex, to satisfy our every need. *I have learned that without God, there is no way you can be fully satisfied.* We often look for validation from things of this world more than validation or the okay from God above. Without God, you will always try to fill a void or have some area in your life of dissatisfaction. You will always feel like there is something missing. Today I want to introduce you to a savior who satisfies and meets your every need. If you are sick, he's a healer. If you are broken, he can mend you back together. If you are lost, he can find you right where you are. If you are down, he can pick you up, no matter how low you may feel you are. If you are an addict, he is a deliverer. He saves, and he satisfies your every need.

\#YouMeetMyEveryNeed

\#IFindItInYou

\#YouSatisfyMe

Prayer

God, there are areas in my life that I feel unsatisfied. Today I give them to you and take refuge in you and allow you to meet my every need. Amen.

Word Workout Plan

Psalm 107:9

Isaiah 58:11

Jeremiah 31:25

Isaiah 55:2

Proverbs 3:5–6

Day 37

Word of the Day

THE POWER OF CONSISTENCY

One day we are hot; the next day, it is cold. One day we are up; the next day, we are down. Some of us struggle with being consistent, behaving the same way every day, having the same frame of mental state. In some point of our lives, we have encountered not being consistent, and it has led us to procrastination, being unfulfilled, laziness, or even being double-minded. *Being consistent is the foundation of self-discipline.* When you apply consistency to your life, you will see the power of consistency manifested through your life. A life that is disciplined is a life that is governed by the power of consistency. Today I challenge you to create healthy, consistent patterns in your life that brings you closer to God, your family, and your purpose. Don't know where to start? Try having a consistent prayer life. It worked for us.

#TheSameEveryday

#SelfDisipline

#IHaveAGoalToReach

Prayer

God, help me not to be up and down but to have a consistent spirit every day. Amen.

Word Workout Plan

Malachi 3:6

Psalm 102:27

James 1:17

Numbers 23:19

1 Samuel 15:29

Day 38

Word of the Day

SHINE A LIGHT ON 'EM

To illuminate something means to shine a light on it and to make it brighter and more visible. In a world that is filled with darkness, God has called us to be the light that's shining so bright that darkness runs away. *When we shine a light on 'em, we are shining hope in a world that is filled with hopelessness.* When we shine a light on 'em, we are shining peace in a world that is filled with fear and anxiety. When we shine a light on 'em, we are giving off rays of love from the Son of God. His love shines through hurt. His love shines through depression. His love even shines through low self-esteem. When you shine a light 'em, darkness has to flee. When you apply the light to situations that are dark in your life, you become a target to be blessed. Blessing will chase you down when you *shine a light on 'em.*

#ShineALightOnEm

#IAmAboutToBeBlessed

#IAmATargertForABlessing

Prayer

God, today I pray for power to access the light and shine my light so that the world will see you and give you glory. Amen.

Word Workout Plan

Psalm 119:105

Matthew 4:16

Matthew 5:16

1 John 1:5–9

Day 39

Word of the Day

CAN'T TOUCH THIS

The plan and the purpose of the enemy is to try and make you feel defeated in every area in your life. He will try to get you to feel oppressed and depressed and to live in fear as a result of life's circumstances. However, I want you to understand that he has no power over your life but what you give to him. God has a hedge of protection all around you, and his angels are encamped about you. You need to tell the devil that he can't touch the plan and the anointing that God has placed on your life. The enemy will always try his best to throw curveballs in your life, but you can't hit a home run with a curveball. He will always try to throw lemons in your life, but when he does, you make lemonade out of those lemons and have yourself a nice glass of lemonade. They whispered and conspired, but they can't touch this because God favored you.

#Can'tTouchThis

#NoWeapon

#NotThisTimeDevil

#IAmSurrounded

Prayer

God, I thank you for the hedge of protection that you placed over me, my family, and my purpose every day. You keep me safe. Amen.

Word Workout Plan

Isaiah 54:17

Job 1:10

Psalm 91:1–16

Psalm 23:1–6

Daniel 6:22

Day 40

Word of the Day

CAN YOU HANDLE THE TRUTH?

We often hear of God's loving-kindness, God's tender mercies, God's grace, and even God's compassion and forgiveness, but at the end of the day, we all are going to have to stand before the righteous judge and give an account for everything we have done. If we are counted worthy, we will enter our eternal resting place called heaven. But if we are not found worthy, *truth is*, there is a place called hell where people who have not lived up to God's expectations and have not confessed that he is Lord over their life go. God loves you so much that he would use a person like me to let you know that today is the day that you can make a complete turnaround and live for him.

The seasoned saints used to say, "Hell is deep. Hell is wide. Hell ain't got no joy inside." You don't think hell is real? You don't think that God is real? You wanna keep doing and living how you want? Well, I got some good, good news for you. In hell, you will lift up your eyes. *This is a warning of love.* Who wants to live eternally out of the presence of God? Can you handle the truth that God is soon to come and we need to get right or prepare for everlasting damnation? God sent the most precious gift that he had so that we would not have to experience hell. Don't let his dying be in vain in your life.

#HeavenIsReal

#HellIsReal

#GetRight

#AWarningOfLove

Prayer

God, today I am turning back to you and everything in my life that is not pleasing to you. I ask that you would help me get rid of it now. I want to be found worthy enough to make it in. Amen.

Word Workout Plan

Revelation 14:10–11

Revelation 22:14–15

Revelation 20:10–15

Mark 9:43–48

Matthew 25:30

John 3:16

Luke 16:19–31

The Salvation Plan

> If you confess with your mouth and believe in your heart that God raised Jesus from the dead, you shall be saved.
>
> —Romans 10:9

God wants to save you!

> Then Peter said to them repent and be baptized everyone of you for the remission of your sins and you shall receive the Holy Spirit. (Acts 2:38)

God wants to clean and fill you!

> For God so loved the world that he gave his only son the whosoever believes in him shall not perish but have everlasting life. (John 3:16)

God wants to redeem you!

Prayer

God, today I give you my life. I give you everything. I believe in your Son, Jesus, that he died and rose for my sins. As of today, I confess you as Lord over my entire life. In Jesus's name, amen.

If you have prayed the prayer of salvation and read the salvation plan, send me an email at Eldersheldonb2810@gmail.com, and I will personally pray with and for you.

I Am a King!

Sheldon Brown

I am a king! I am strong!

I am black! I stand for righteousness!

I am royalty! I am the anointed of God!

I am smart! I am intelligent!

I spew wisdom from my lips.

I won't be overcome by evil, but I will overcome evil with good!

I stand tall! I stand proud!

My drip is on point! I stand bold!

I stand courageous! I am on my grind!

I am a king! I am strong!

I am black! I am a king!

And there's nothing you can do about that!

Acknowledgments

> For we know that all things work together for the good. To them who love the lord and are called according to his purpose.
> —Romans 8:28

This is the scripture that has supported my every accomplishment and failure. I want to give all glory and honor to God for every mountain he has brought me over, every valley he's seen me though.

To my beautiful queen of eleven years, Michelle Brown; my three kings—Zion, Zaire, and Zuriel—and my little prince, Zayden, thank you for all your love and support in everything. Through the good, the bad and the ugly, FAST (family always sticks together) has been our learned motivation.

I want to thank my mother, Sherita Brown, and my father, Melvin Brown, for all their love and support and prayers my whole life.

I want to thank my good friend Tammy Caesar for her prayers, many prophecies, love, and support.

I want to thank my evangelist Arleta Lee for being my pusher and my prayer partner for years.

I want to give God praise for Dr. Kadjiah Harris Campbell for her many countless hours and dedication to my family and me.

To my best friends, Min Nathan Willey and Prophet Benjamin Horton, thank you guys for all your motivational talks and prayers and even fussing over me when I needed it. LOL.

To all the apostles, bishops, prophets, evangelists, ministers, elders, and people of the most high God who have prayed and labored for me, thank you.

To all my family, thank you for your love and support.

For Booking

Contact Assistant Michelle Brown at 443-942-0257.

Contact Sheldon Brown at 410-725-0273, Eldersheldonb2810@gamil.com, or on Facebook.

CPSIA information can be obtained
at www.ICGtesting.com
Printed in the USA
BVHW030307011221
622919BV00004B/16/J